TABLE MOUNTAIN
and the Cape Peninsula

Christiaan Diedericks
Catherine Eden

Introduction   9

THE FRONT FACE   12
   The Circle of Islam   16
   Table Mountain Aerial Cableway   20
   Tafelberg Road   24
   The City Bowl   26
   Table Bay   30
   Fire Fighting   32

ATLANTIC SEABOARD   34
   Clifton   38
   Camps Bay   40
   Bakoven   44
   Oudekraal   46
   Sandy Bay   50

CHAPMAN'S PEAK & SURROUNDS   52
   Hout Bay   54
   Chapman's Peak   56
   Noordhoek   58
   Noordhoek Valley   60
   Kommetjie, Witsand & Misty Cliffs   64
   Scarborough   68

CONTENTS

CAPE POINT 70
    Cape of Good Hope 72

FALSE BAY 82
    Boulders 84
    Simon's Town 86
    Fish Hoek 88
    Kalk Bay 90
    St James 92
    Muizenberg 94

CONSTANTIA VALLEY 96
    Ou Kaapse Weg & Silvermine 98
    Steenberg 100
    Constantia 102

KIRSTENBOSCH TO DEVIL'S PEAK 108
    Kirstenbosch 112
    Rhodes Memorial 116
    Groote Schuur Estate 118

Index 122
Acknowledgements 127
Through the Photographer's Window 128

Introduction

Table Mountain's familiar outline is the defining characteristic of Cape Town and the symbol of home to all her citizens. In the dark days of apartheid Nelson Mandela described it as 'a beacon of hope' to political prisoners on Robben Island. In post-apartheid South Africa, people still find its reassuring bulk a source of comfort and inspiration.

When the wind blows and a snowy 'tablecloth' billows along the edge of the table, its front face provides an unbeatable backdrop to down-town bustle. But just a few minutes' drive reveals other, equally beautiful faces. On all sides, the mountain offers security, sanctuary and a scenic splendour that takes even the locals by surprise.

Where in the world is there another national park of such diversity and richness right in the heart of a major city? Pristine beaches, secluded forests and rocky hiking trails are a stone's throw from the business district. Beside a roaring freeway, zebra and wildebeest graze peacefully on a hillside overlooking one of the busiest hospitals in the world. And at Boulders beach, protected penguins put their babies to bed right beside the picnic baskets.

White sand, blue sea and big, big skies are part of Cape Town's profile, but it is Hoerikwaggo – a Khoisan word meaning 'sea mountain' – that shapes its exceptional natural beauty, supports an abundance of animal and bird life, and forms part of one of the greatest floral kingdoms in the world.

To visitors, Table Mountain is a compelling presence whose call must be obeyed, but to Capetonians it is simply 'The Mountain': unchanging, eternal and beloved above all others.

THE FRONT FACE

Table Mountain, Hoerikwaggo, Umlindi Wemingizimu, Taboa do Cabo: Cape Town's greatest asset has had many names. It is not remarkable for its height (1 088 m), but positioned as it is, with one of the world's most celebrated cities at its feet, it is incomparable. If Cape Town is the Mother City, Table Mountain is her heart. From the top there's a view of toy-town skyscrapers and the harbour, rubbing shoulders with the glamorous Victoria and Alfred Waterfront. Visiting tankers sit at anchor in Table Bay, and Robben Island, free at last of its political taint, rises above the water. The stresses of city life are tempered by the constant example of the mountain, where clouds build and then evaporate into tendrils of mist.

The Circle of Islam

After Bartolomeu Dias opened the sea route to the east in 1488, the Cape of Good Hope became a vital port for supplies of fresh food and water. The Dutch East India Company sent Jan van Riebeeck to establish a permanent settlement at the Cape in 1652, with orders not to enslave the indigenous Khoisan people (estimated to number fewer than 8 000 at the time). Slaves were brought from West Africa instead, and later from Madagascar and the East Indies. Dissenters sent into exile from Dutch colonies were added to the mix, and one of these, Sheik Yusuf, brought Islam to the Cape in 1693. The faith and culture is now an integral part of the Cape Town tapestry. In the steep streets of the Bo-Kaap in particular, the call of the muezzin echoes at dawn, and spicy aromas waft from the deep doorways of narrow houses painted in saffron, ochre and rose. The mountain has been a holy burial place for many in the history of the Cape. This **kramat** (OPPOSITE) on the slopes of **Lion's Head** (SEE FOLLOWING PAGE, LEFT) is one of six graves that form a Circle of Islam on the Peninsula. It is believed that those living within the circle are protected from natural disasters.

Table Mountain Aerial Cableway

The 1 200-m cableway opened in 1929, and to date has carried more than 13 million passengers. The system was upgraded in 1997 and now has spacious cars that rotate completely as they make the roughly five-minute climb to the **upper cable station** (PREVIOUS SPREAD). They carry a maximum load of 65 passengers and 4 000 litres of water contained in a tank in the floor of the cabin.

The water provides stability in the wind, and in fine weather is supplied to the restaurant. The hardy, or those who suffer from vertigo, may prefer the slow and rather taxing hike to the top, following one of the established routes. The first recorded climb was in 1503 by Portuguese Admiral Antonia de Saldanha, who afterwards felt entitled to rename the Khoisan's 'Hoerikwaggo' to 'Taboa do Cabo', meaning Table of the Cape.

On foot or by cable car, the trip is a must. It's surprisingly cold up there, but the views are spectacular. On one hand, the west coast winds out of sight; on the other, the sea wraps round the craggy shoreline, bordering white beaches with bands of turquoise and blue.

Table Mountain was declared a national monument in 1958, but its name was written in the stars long ago. Mons Mensa ('table mountain') is a constellation close to the Southern Cross and the Cloud of Magellan, whose milky haze echoes the famous table cloth. Water is scarce in the dry summer months when the south-easterly 'Cape Doctor' blasts the city clean of smog, but nature provides for the mountain: vegetation receives more water from cloud moisture than it does from rain. The cloud can come down in minutes, taking

hikers by surprise and sending the diurnal rock hyrax or 'dassie' scurrying for cover. The dassie's claim to fame is that it is the elephant's closest relative. Well adapted to its rocky habitat, it has sticky pads on its feet and a collapsible ribcage that allows it to squeeze into narrow crevices to escape from danger. A siren sounds at the upper cable station and **restaurant** (ABOVE) to warn visitors of approaching bad weather or when it is necessary to return to the cable car.

Tafelberg Road

Winding along the front face of the mountain, Tafelberg Road provides access to the lower cable station and, at its furthest end, to the slopes of Devil's Peak. According to folklore, a retired pirate named Van Hunks is said to have passed his days there, smoking his pipe. Van Hunks challenged the devil to a competition and produced such volumes of smoke that to this day, when clouds billow above the peak (SEE PAGE 118, CENTRE), locals comment, 'Van Hunks is smoking his pipe again.' A path leads to the King's blockhouse, constructed in 1790 as a lookout post over Table Bay but used instead to house prisoners who were assigned to planting trees on the mountainside.

Development on all sides of Table Mountain makes it one of the world's few national parks to be found in the centre of a bustling city, allowing walkers, runners and cyclists quick and easy access to forests, beaches and mountain paths.

Floodlights just above Tafelberg Road illuminate the mountain at night for part of the year, as can be seen from **Lion's Head** (SEE PAGES 14–15).

 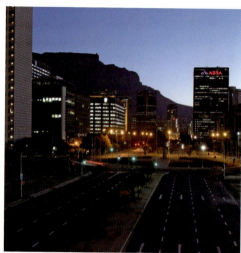 

The City Bowl

As the noon gun booms, birds briefly take flight over the City Bowl, which rests between the sea and the mountain slopes that sweep from Devil's Peak to Signal Hill.

Merged with modern constructions are architectural remnants of the past: gabled façades from the Dutch and Georgian elegance from the British. Part of Cape Town's charm is its mix of commercial and community life: downtown bustle blended with the settled shadows of the **Bo-Kaap** (OPPOSITE) and the lively districts of De Waterkant and Gardens.

The **Mount Nelson Hotel** (ABOVE, RIGHT) remains one of the city's best-loved colonial relics, where wild teatime fantasies are realised. Well-heeled tourists stroll down leafy Government Avenue to the Company Gardens, where hydrangeas bloom in the shade and children coax nervous squirrels to eat peanuts out of their hands.

As you look back from **Adderley Street** (ABOVE, CENTRE), the mountain seems close enough to touch. There's evidence of progress all over town, but the essence of Cape Town is a distillation of the things that never change.

Table Bay

To appreciate its full splendour, Cape Town is best approached from the sea. In the days of leisurely ocean crossings families gathered at the **harbour** (ABOVE, LEFT) to watch tugboats nudge great liners away from the quay. Tinny loudspeakers blared 'The Skye Boat Song', and fragile streamers unfurled in colourful arcs from ship to eager hands on shore, only to stretch, snap, and subside in the water.

The city still has a hard-working harbour and heavy traffic in Table Bay, but it has also developed a glamorous side that attracts traffic of a different kind. The **V&A Waterfront** (ABOVE, RIGHT) is a tourist's paradise of restaurants and shop-till-you-drop stores in an extraordinarily picturesque and vibrant setting. Ferries to Robben Island depart from the **Nelson Mandela Gateway** (PREVIOUS SPREAD), and charter boats at Quay Four offer harbour and sunset cruises. As you sail round the breakwater, there is the slap of the silvery swell and the hiss of salt spray; and, if you are lucky, a brief ballet performed by a duo of dolphins. When the bubbly comes round, take it, because this is a sight to be celebrated.

Fire Fighting

Fire occurs frequently in the park area, destroying acres of vegetation that has been sucked dry by the relentless summer sun. Although it can be devastating, fire is a natural part of the cycle of the Cape's indigenous flora (known as fynbos), triggering germination in some plants. At least 2 200 species have been recorded in the Table Mountain National Park, but many are on the endangered list and others are threatened by fast-growing alien vegetation that was introduced to the Cape by misguided colonists as early as the 1700s.

After a serious fire in January 2000, 'Ukuvuka, Operation Firestop' was launched to rid the mountain of aliens, repair the landscape and help protect vulnerable communities living on the fringes of the park. Clearing of invasive alien vegetation has created many jobs, particularly for previously disadvantaged citizens. The war is waged on three fronts: hacking, chemical sprays and the use of biological agents.

Cape Town's well-trained firefighters are supported by helicopters standing by at the forestry station at Newlands, ready to respond to fires at a moment's notice.

ATLANTIC SEABOARD

If the front face of the mountain looms over the city's cosmopolitan, nine-to-five workplace, the Twelve Apostles preside benignly over its playground. This is the Atlantic seaboard – the glitz and glamour strip of the park where the young and beautiful gather for sundowners, the wealthy bask on priceless beach-front terraces and adrenalin junkies paraglide off the top of Lion's Head or spin across the glinting water clinging to colourful surf kites. Some of the country's most spectacular beaches are on this stretch of coastline at Llandudno, Bakoven, Camps Bay and Clifton. The mountain range actually numbers 15 buttresses, none of which has an Apostle's name. Sir Rufane Donkin, Governor of the Cape in 1820, settled on the Twelve Apostles misnomer in preference to the Dutch De Gevelbergen, meaning 'Gable Mountains'.

Atlantic seaboard

Not many places offer forest, beach and mountain pursuits in a 15-minute radius from the city centre. After a stressful day at work city dwellers may walk on **Clifton Beach** (ABOVE, RIGHT) to blow the cobwebs away, or drive to Signal Hill to enjoy the view. For the after-work dog-walking brigade, the evening ritual of a trip to the shady Glen has developed into an enjoyable social occasion. While Rufus and Romeo chase sticks, their owners combine gentle exercise with endless networking opportunities.

The 669-m hike up **Lion's Head** (ABOVE, CENTRE) is relatively easy, with a certain amount of scrambling in places. Chains are set into the rock at a steep point in the route, but there is the option of a longer, more gradual detour to avoid the climb. (Lion's Head, which really couldn't be called anything else, apparently had a brief incarnation as 'Ye Sugar Loafe' in the 1620s. Fortunately, the name didn't stick.) The climb is particularly popular at full moon, when groves of shimmering silver trees mirror the gleam on the sea far below.

Clifton

The famous four at Clifton must rate among the world's best-known beaches. Demarcated by rocky outcrops, each expanse of soft white sand has its own character and its regular devotees who come to socialise, to see and be seen, or just to revive in the glorious surroundings. Five-star apartment blocks cling to the mountainside and steep stairways leading from the beaches to street level thread through a rabbit warren of homes that have morphed from modest beach shacks into some of the most expensive real estate in the country.

Only the hardy take to water that is notoriously cold, even in summer. It's much more comfortable to view the Clifton beach scene and its extravagant backdrop from the deck of a cruise boat boarded at the V&A Waterfront.

As the setting sun casts a pink and vermillion wash on the clouds, picnickers open their baskets and settle candles in the still-warm sand, to be lit when the last of the colours has faded.

Camps Bay

Pleasure-seekers jam the roads leading to Camps Bay's palm-lined beachfront – the setting for designer salads and sundowners, volleyball games and sociable gatherings. The white sand is usually sprinkled with sun worshippers, but high tide conjures a shallow lagoon where children paddle and aspirant surfers take their first wobbly ride. Pavement cafés and restaurants stand shoulder to shoulder overlooking the water, with the suburb's residential streets crowded behind them. In a flash-back to the colonial past, games of cricket and bowls play out on the nearby greens.

Camps Bay was known as Roodekrantz when Dutch governor Jan van Riebeeck bestowed it on John Lodewyk Wernich in the late 17th century. After his death his widow married Frederik Ernst von Kamptz whose name was given to the district. Once the British had defeated the Dutch in 1806 at Blouberg, Governor Sir Charles Somerset took to hunting in Camps Bay, using the Round House as his lodge. By 1848 Lady Smith's Pass (later renamed Kloof Road) had been built, putting Camps Bay firmly on the map.

The Camps Bay strip has something for everyone. For the sedentary there's the appeal of a sunset beach picnic in a million-dollar setting that's only a few level metres away from the car. For the moderately fit there's the pleasant walk along the **pipe track** (OPPOSITE), where the Cape's indigenous fynbos competes with alien pines on the slopes above the densely populated suburb. And for lovers of extreme sports, there's the irresistible allure of kite-surfing and paragliding.

Fine weather drives the intrepid to leap off **Lion's Head** (ABOVE, LEFT) and ride the thermals for as long as possible before swooping out of the sky to make impressive and colourful landings on the grassy doorstep of a popular outdoor café.

From the lion's spine there's an exceptional view of the city on one flank, and the bright lights of Camps Bay on the other. With palm trees and piña coladas, and turquoise water lapping at a sandy white shore, who needs the Caribbean? On fine evenings city slickers turn out to enjoy seaside pleasures, revelling in the right to call this place home.

Bakoven

Massive boulders dwarf visitors to Bakoven, where a tiny, tucked-away beach serves the lucky few who live here – as close to the sea as it is possible to get. On calm days sea kayaks nose round the sheltered bays, but when the wind whips up the water it's only the frothy 'white horses' that can be seen cresting the waves.

Bakoven is the last stop on the busy Camps Bay drag. Beyond it, the coastal road abruptly shakes off its party clothes and runs unhindered through relatively untouched landscape in the direction of Llandudno and Hout Bay. Victoria Road was built by Thomas Bain in 1848 and named for Queen Victoria in honour of her jubilee. The road carves into a mountainside of Table Mountain sandstone that meets the sea on a ragged, stony shoreline that's claimed many an unwary ship as it ploughs through the water on its way to Cape Point.

Oudekraal

Three Muslim graves stand on the hillside at Oudekraal. One is the resting place of Sheik Noorul Mubeen, exiled to the Cape in the early 1700s and imprisoned on Robben Island. Legend has it that he escaped by strange means and made his way to the mainland, where he began teaching slaves in the area about Islam.

Public emotion has run high ever since the Administrator of the Cape made an unfortunate ruling in 1957 that this ecologically and spiritually sensitive land could be developed into an elite residential area. In 1992 a **hotel and conference centre** (ABOVE, RIGHT) were built on the privately owned site, amid great controversy. The debate was finally resolved in 2004 when Appeal Court judges overturned the 1957 ruling as invalid, thereby saving the land from further development.

Oudekraal is famous for its established milkwood trees that knot a gnarled canopy over pathways plunging down to secret coves and a perfect sliver of beach, where divers suit up to explore protected corals and abundant marine life.

Sandy Bay

Architects' flights of fancy perch on the ultra-desirable slopes at **Llandudno** (PREVIOUS SPREAD), where perfect sunsets are commonplace and where a secluded beach provides that away-from-it-all experience offered by exotic holiday destinations. From Llandudno a path leads through the bush for about two kilometres, opening on to the remote nudist beach at Sandy Bay where the constraints of the city

– and the need to wear clothes – are cast to the wind. Excavations in 1954 at Llandudno's Logie's Rock Cave revealed a shell midden containing flaked stone tools, ostrich eggshell beads, bone tubes and points, as well as ochre-stained upper grindstones, indicating that the Khoisan enjoyed this pristine coastline long before Van Riebeeck claimed the Cape. By the early 18th century the Khoisan were gone: some trekked inland, but most were hunted and killed, or wiped out by smallpox introduced by the newcomers.

CHAPMAN'S PEAK
& SURROUNDS

The wildest face of Table Mountain includes the fishing hamlet of Hout Bay, spectacular Chapman's Peak Drive, and the moody, windswept beaches at Noordhoek, Kommetjie and Scarborough. John Chapman, master's mate on the English ship *The Consent* was sent ashore one day in 1607 to search for fresh water. The bay he explored was known as 'Chapman's Chaunce' but changed to 'Hout Bay' after Van Riebeeck, who visited the area nearly 50 years later, enthused about the impressive forests of ''t Houtbaaitjen'. Modern Hout Bay brims with attitude: a publicity stunt to declare the valley a 'republic' ignited patriotic fervour that had residents queuing for passports to prove their citizenship.

Hout Bay

The distinctive **Sentinel** (OPPOSITE) guards the entrance to Hout Bay, a popular seaside honeymoon destination at the end of the 19th century. It had a hotel, a church and a fledgling fishing industry that boomed in the 1930s when the working harbour was built and a system for transporting fresh fish was devised.

A sculpted leopard sits on a rock in tribute to the wild animals that roamed the deeply forested wilderness before 18th century conflict between the British and the Dutch brought heavy **cannon** to the bay (ABOVE, RIGHT). Now no more than a novelty, they co-exist with modern **fishing boats** (ABOVE, CENTRE) and pleasure cruisers that offer sunset jaunts along the coastline. As cyclists spin down Suikerbossie hill, the view across the valley takes in sprawling **Imizamo Yethu**, also known as Mandela Park (ABOVE, LEFT), an initiative aimed at creating a stable community for squatters drawn to the area by employment opportunities at the harbour. Tours of the settlement generate income for guides, choirs and craftsmen, and expand business prospects outside the community.

Chapman's Peak

Carving a road into the shale that separates the granite base from the upper layers of sandstone on Chapman's Peak was a dangerous, painstaking feat of engineering that lasted from 1915 to 1922.

In January 2000, after a series of rock falls and fires destabilised the ground above the road, it was closed for extensive repairs and improvements. The work took four years to complete and the results are impressive: massive nets slung between gigantic iron stakes have been installed at likely rock-fall points; upper slopes have been secured and half tunnels and canopy structures have been constructed on the most vulnerable bends.

The route was re-opened at the end of 2003 as a toll road. Always a showpiece for its awesome splendour, Chapman's Peak is of even greater interest to visitors now, thanks to the dramatic safety features that qualify as an attraction in their own right. Even with these precautions in place, the drive may be closed in bad weather or after severe rock-falls.

Noordhoek

Chapman's Peak Drive links Hout Bay with the tranquil village of Noordhoek, whose vast and lonely stretch of beach can be viewed from the serpentine curves of the pass. Horses from the nearby stables come down to the sea to cool off, and walkers can tramp along the shore for hours. Even in a group (advisable in this remote location) it's impossible to feel crowded in such a wild and beautiful

setting where a rusted wreck emerging from the sand is a reminder of the ships that have succumbed to the notorious Cape of Storms. The Silvermine Nature Reserve, which sweeps into the valley, takes its name from a fruitless attempt to extract silver from the mountain in 1687. A project started in 1909 to mine manganese in Hout Bay was similarly unsatisfactory and the mine was closed two years later. The only viable mine in a region poorly supplied with mineral deposits is the kaolin mine at Noordhoek.

Noordhoek Valley

The low-lying land in the Kommetjie district is an important wetland that links the southern and the northern parts of the Table Mountain National Park. Before 2002, when 450 hectares were incorporated into the Park's area of jurisdiction, the land was a neglected swamp choked with invasive alien vegetation. Restoring it to its natural state has provided indigenous flora and fauna with a supportive habitat.

Noordhoek and Kommetjie have also become the habitat of creative people who choose to practise their crafts in this unhurried corner of the Peninsula. Potters and artists of all kinds open their studios to visitors following the valley's art route, or supply their creations to shops in the farm village complex. A stroll under the oaks, with vivid peacocks or portly turkeys strutting by, conjures images of a mostly long-forgotten lifestyle. Horses graze in English-style paddocks; and hot scones drip with home-made preserves and dollops of thick, fresh cream in a farm-stall tearoom smelling of baskets. There's also the novelty of a camel ride at Imhoff farm, or game viewing at the Solole Buffalo Reserve.

Kommetjie, Witsand & Misty Cliffs

The **Slangkop Lighthouse** (PREVIOUS SPREAD) cuts a lonely figure on the inhospitable stretch of shore near Kommetjie, and wind whistles across the wild, exposed beach at **Witsand** (ABOVE). Although swimming is risky, the beaches in the area attract surfers and steel-nerved **sailboarders** (FOLLOWING SPREAD) who skim over the waves in such a way that they become airborne. The colourful sails appear to dance

effortlessly over the water – until they crash, tossing their pilots into the foam like matchsticks. Struggling to shore is exhausting, but the exhilaration of the ride keeps them coming back for more. The small **Misty Cliffs** settlement (FOLLOWING SPREAD) climbs into the narrow gorge overlooking the beach. A project to declare this area a conservation village has focused on ridding it of alien vegetation and returning it, as far as possible, to its natural state. As its name suggests, it becomes a mysterious, almost spooky place when the mist rolls in.

Scarborough

Time stands still in the village of Scarborough, where the community is made up largely of self-supporting creative individuals, retired folk and holiday makers who fill up the guest houses and B&B establishments in the summer season. Being so far from the beaten track, it's the place to go for a rest cure, or to write a novel, or to escape from a life that's become overwhelming. A Sunday drive to Scarborough,

a cold beer in its invigorating atmosphere overlooking Camel Rock – the defining feature of the village – and the chance to recall the playfulness of childhood by building a sandcastle on the beach acts like a tonic on the frazzled nerves of high-density city dwellers. Baboons are often spotted in this part of the world. Because of the potential for conflict between home-owners and foraging baboon troops, monitors have been appointed to keep an eye on the animals' movements and take steps where necessary to avert trouble.

CAPE POINT

Sir Francis Drake, the swashbuckling 16th century English adventurer credited with being the first to circumnavigate the globe, declared this 'the fairest cape in the whole circumference of the earth'. Although the Greek historian Herodotus suggests that the Phoenicians sailed these waters as long ago as 600 BC, modern history books credit the Portuguese explorer Bartolomeu Dias with opening the sea route between Europe and the east in 1488.

Cape of Good Hope

The reserve at the tip of Table Mountain National Park once supported fishing, whaling and lime-making, but even after the road from Simon's Town was completed in the first decade of the 20th century it was so remote that parts of it could only be reached by sea.

The 1859 lighthouse, positioned 238 m above sea level, was set so high and so far inland that its beam was often lost in the mist that shrouds these cliffs. The new **lighthouse** (OPPOSITE), built just 87.8 m above the water has a candlepower of 10 million, making it the strongest light on the South African coastline, visible from a distance of 63 km.

The crosses commemorating Bartolomeu Dias and his countryman **Vasco da Gama** (ABOVE, LEFT) stand in a landscape that has barely changed since they made their historic voyages. Visitors to the 7 750-ha reserve come for the crisp silence, the views and the abundance of indigenous flora for which the Cape is world renowned. The reserve has a number of walks, a two-day hiking trail, and is the end destination of the six-night Hoerikwaggo Trail from Cape Town.

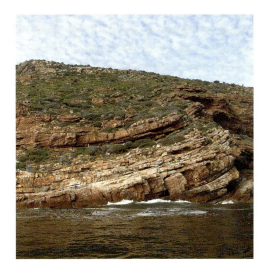  

In the 1700s, Sultan Kaharuddin (known also as 'Antonie' or 'The Tuan of Antonie's Gat') was exiled to the Cape for participating in a plot to overthrow Dutch rule on the Indonesian island of Sumbawa. He escaped from prison and lived out his life in one of the sea-level **caves at Cape Point** (OPPOSITE and ABOVE), where those who come by boat to pay their respects claim to have occasionally seen his ghost.

Better documented is the ghost of *The Flying Dutchman*, wrecked off the coast in 1641. She is said to roam the sea, hailing passing ships, but none will respond for fear of encountering a similar fate.

Cape Point is undeniably dramatic, and the clashing of currents in the turbulent zone known as 'the washing machine' suggests that it is the meeting place of two mighty oceans. Capetonians are divided on the issue, with purists pointing out that the most southerly point of Africa is 150 km east at Cape Agulhas, and romantics insisting that the warm waters of False Bay are part of the Indian Ocean, since distinctly different marine life occurs on either side of the point.

A brief roadside stop in the reserve is likely to reward the observant visitor with sightings of a colourful **erica** (ABOVE, CENTRE) – an important member of the fynbos group – a low-slung grey mongoose, a ponderous tortoise and, out in the breakers, a solitary seal playing to an imaginary audience. In the distance eland graze metres from the shore, and flocks of **seabirds** swoop over the shallows near **Buffels Bay** (PREVIOUS SPREAD). A chorus line of **ostriches** may appear, extending ridiculous necks against a backdrop of bright blue sea (FOLLOWING SPREAD).

Baboons are bound to get in on the act, and at this point the visitor should retreat to the car. Although **Chacma baboons** (ABOVE, RIGHT) are found throughout southern Africa, advancing urban sprawl has isolated troops in the Cape Peninsula, where they are now endangered. Baboons feed largely on fynbos, but the animals in the Cape Point area are most unusual in that they have learned to forage along the shore for mussels, limpets and shark egg embryos. Tourists encountering baboons are tempted to feed them but, in doing so, they sign the animals' death warrant. Not only is unsuitable food harmful to them, but once they acquire a taste for it they can adopt aggressive tactics to get to it, and may have to be destroyed.

FALSE BAY

When explorers of old sailed into False Bay, many were tricked into thinking the Cape had been rounded. The bay takes a huge bite into the land between Cape Point and Cape Hangklip, sweeping from Simon's Town and **Muizenberg** (ABOVE, scene of the 1795 battle that ended 150 years of Dutch rule) to Gordon's Bay and Pringle Bay on the opposite coast. False Bay shelters the famous penguin colony at Boulders, and the Southern Right whales who come here to calve. Great White sharks cruise these waters too, feeding off the abundant seal population. Tidal pools, Victorian bathing boxes and faded elegance characterise the relaxed face of the mountain where trek fishermen on Fish Hoek beach haul nets as their forefathers did, and boats laden with the catch of the day return to picturesque Kalk Bay harbour.

Boulders

Of the world's 17 penguin species, only one visits African shores. The African Penguin (previously known as the Jackass Penguin), breeds from Namibia to Algoa Bay in the Eastern Cape. Colonies are usually located offshore, where birds are less vulnerable during the moulting season when lack of waterproofing prevents them from taking to the sea, but at Boulders beach near Simon's Town these comical creatures toddle among the picnic baskets and share their sheltered cove with human swimmers.

Boulders is one of only three mainland colonies, housing a population that has grown to over 3 000 since the first breeding pair was spotted in 1984. Penguins live for approximately 10 years, breeding between March and May. Attentive parents can be seen settling their offspring into sandy nests on the shore as the sun goes down.

After a devastating oil spill drenched thousands of penguins, Capetonians rallied in an unprecedented community effort to wash, feed and transport them up the coast to clean water. Penguin veterans of oil spills wear data tags that help researchers monitor the population.

Simon's Town

This charming town became a South African naval base in 1957, after 143 years of British control. Its colonial past is reflected in architecture on the 'historic mile' and in the intricate 'broekie lace' that adorns gracious homes overlooking the dockyard and yacht basin. Beyond the harbour, unusual Nelson's Rock lighthouse emerges from the sea.

A statue on Jubilee Square honours Just Nuisance, a Great Dane who was given the rank of Able Seaman for guiding drunken sailors back to the hostel after a night on the town.

In the 1700s the Dutch Governor spent winters at The Residency (now Simon's Town Museum) which was also a prison to the likes of Antonie (SEE PAGE 75) and his younger brother Ismail, who eventually settled in the town with his wife, a slave from St Helena. Slaves outnumbered settlers at the time of the second British occupation in 1805, but the practice of slavery was officially abolished in the Cape on 1 December 1834.

The population of Simon's Town is a blend of Khoisan, African and Asian slaves, settlers, Indians and Lithuanian Jews. They shaped the town's history, and their presence lingers.

Fish Hoek

***Trek* fishing** (ABOVE) is an institution at Fish Hoek – a gem of a beach that amply makes up for the architectural inadequacies of a town whose main claim to fame is a policy forbidding the sale of alcohol in its precincts. When a scout situated at the mountain lookout post gives the signal (cell phone technology has replaced the old mirror-flashing technique), the fishermen scramble into fat-bellied boats

and row out beyond the breakers. Nets are cast, and then painstakingly hauled in by teams of sinewy men. They are assisted by tourists and locals who love the ritual and the fact that supper can be bought straight from the nets. The concrete 'catwalk', with the single train line running above, follows the coast to Sunny Cove. Regulars still swim in the deep water off the rocks, despite the possibility of a deadly attack from one of the Great White sharks that are commonly sighted in False Bay.

Kalk Bay

The Bohemian side of the mountain is expressed in the shabby chic of Kalk Bay, a fishing village frequented by highbrows and hoboes who inhale the same salt air blowing off the waves that roll beyond the harbour wall. This is the place for antiquarian books and 'collectables' of all sorts, made more desirable by intriguing alleyways, bright boats bobbing on blue water and the prospect of fresh-baked croissants from the bakery.

Generations of fishermen have lived in Kalk Bay, but the established community has mushroomed to include escapees from the city who've opted for the laid-back village lifestyle. A dip at Dalebrook tidal pool, coffee at the deli and a stroll along the pier sets anyone up for the day. Several popular restaurants attract patrons from far and wide, who come to enjoy fish so fresh that it's almost flapping on the plate.

On the mountain, Boyes Drive provides the perfect panoramic view of False Bay. Visitors stop to count whales in the spring, and hikers and cave enthusiasts strike further up the hillside to explore the network of paths and underground tunnels and caverns.

St James

For anyone who has grown up in the False Bay region, the gently sloping **tidal pool** at St James (OPPOSITE) is indelibly associated with summer holidays and sunshiny weekends. There are rock pools to explore and shells to collect, and every now and then there's the drama of the train thundering by. The **railway** to Simon's Town (ABOVE, LEFT) runs so close to the shore at this point that heavy seas sometimes spray the tracks.

When the whales come in August people gather on the rocky outcrops to watch them blowing and thwacking their great tails on the water. Southern Rights were so called because this species (*Eubalaena australis*) was considered 'right' to kill as it floated when harpooned and supplied quantities of blubber, meat and bone. Roughly 12 000 were butchered between 1785 and 1805, and by 1940 when they became protected in South African waters there were only about 50 breeding females migrating to False Bay. Happily, the population doubles every decade and has now swelled to a healthy number. Humpback, Bryde's and Killer whales are also seen; as are Common, Dusky and Bottlenosed dolphins.

Muizenberg

Colourful wooden **bathing boxes** at Muizenberg (OPPOSITE) have become a defining image of the False Bay coastline. **Boyes Drive** (ABOVE, LEFT) overlooks long lines of breakers and the once fashionable seaside town. There are hints of its past grandeur in the palatial, peeling buildings, in the rejuvenated Empire Theatre and in the red-brick splendour of the old station house, topped with a decorative turret. Historic buildings in the area include the little whitewashed and thatched **Het Posthuys Museum** (ABOVE, CENTRE), containing a display of the battle of Muizenberg; the sumptuous Natale Labia gallery, and the unassuming cottage (now a museum) which Cecil John Rhodes used as a holiday home and where he died on 26 March 1902, apparently to the accompaniment of thunderous surf on the beach.

When the surf is not too overpowering, it's possible to walk from Muizenberg to Kalk Bay on a path that runs between the railway line and the water. Across the road the ever-present mountain squeezes houses into a narrow band, as if planning to push them into the sea.

CONSTANTIA VALLEY

The Constantia Valley is the tranquil, sylvan face of the mountain, known for its wine, its wealth and its wide open spaces. Before the property boom that began in the 1980s much of it was rural. Even though there has been extensive development in the last two decades, green belts run like arteries through the neighbourhoods, supplying fresh air, birdsong and beauty. Constantiaberg and **Elephant's Eye** (ABOVE) overlook working farms where gracious homesteads in the Cape Dutch style stand among oak trees and lush green vineyards.

  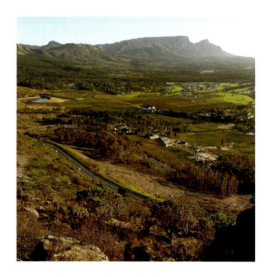

Ou Kaapse Weg & Silvermine

The old mountain pass that linked Constantia farms with early coastal outposts is still in use today. At its highest point **Ou Kaapse Weg** (ABOVE, LEFT) cuts through the **Silvermine Nature Reserve** (ABOVE, CENTRE AND RIGHT), providing an exceptional view of the fertile valley sweeping towards False Bay. As the route drops away on the other side, fynbos wraps around rocky terrain that changes its mood according to the season: bleak and misty in winter; baking and alive with the song of cicadas in summer. Fire regularly scorches these hills, turning them into a barren moonscape. But they can just as quickly flower with flame-coloured Erica blooms and splashes of purple and white.

Cyclists train on the steep bends for the Argus Cycle Tour, which attracts thousands of competitors to the Peninsula to participate in the world's largest timed cycle race. As the road snakes down to the Noordhoek valley, False Bay is visible on the left, and the cold Atlantic shoreline on the right. Stands of invasive vegetation meet their match in the form of roadside woodcutters who sell neat towers of logs in preparation for the winter chill.

Steenberg

The silhouette of the mountain chain forms a splendid backdrop to the **Westlake** (ABOVE, CENTRE) and **Steenberg golf courses** (ABOVE, LEFT AND RIGHT). A communications mast marks the highest point of **Constantiaberg** (OPPOSITE) which drops away to Constantia Nek and the region's winelands. The first owner of Steenberg was Catharina Michelse, an adventurous German who came to the Cape in 1662 as a 22-year-old widow. Her second husband was eaten by a lion, the third was murdered, and the fourth was trampled by an elephant. The last, Matthys Michelse, was a fellow German with staying power. In 1688 Catharina was granted a title deed and a mandate to 'cultivate, to plough, to sow and also to possess the farm below the stone mountain'. She called it 'Swaaneweide', the feeding place of swans, although the only bird resembling a swan at the time would have been a spur-winged goose. Frederik Russouw bought the farm in 1695, and produced its first wines. It changed hands a number of times before it was bought by a developer in the 1990s and extensively remodelled to include new vineyards, a hotel and a **golf village** (OPPOSITE).

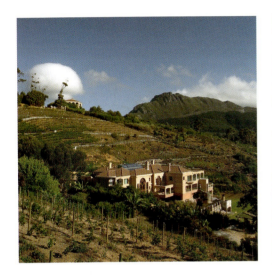  

Constantia

Simon van der Stel, third Governor of the Cape, was granted nearly 2 500 ha of land in 1685 for the production of fruit and vegetables needed by ships en route to the East. This vast estate was divided into three sections in 1716: modern Bergvliet, Klein Constantia and Groot Constantia, where the much-visited manor house still stands. The homestead was badly damaged by fire in 1925 but was restored, furnished and preserved as a museum that offers visitors an experience of mid-17th century Cape Dutch style. Groot Constantia may be the best known of the valley's original wine farms, but other examples of this distinctive architecture can also be seen at **Buitenverwagting** (OPPOSITE), **Steenberg** (ABOVE, RIGHT), Klein Constantia and Uitsig.

It's hard to top the elegance and incomparable setting of these historic homes, but modern Constantia does its best to rise to the challenge. Opulent palaces rear up beside unpretentious paddocks, earning the region the reputation of being Cape Town's 'mink and manure' belt.

The farms and vineyards on the valley's wine route have diversified to include gift shops, restaurants, wine tasting and leisure facilities to entice visitors to the area. Capetonians are spoilt for choice: it's possible to walk the dog at Groot Constantia, play golf at Steenberg, taste a perfect Sauvignon Blanc at Klein Constantia, lunch at Uitsig and pick an armful of roses at **Chart farm** (ABOVE) in the space of a single day.

For all its up-market shopping and residential splendour, Constantia remains a quiet part of Cape Town where bird life is rich and the air is sweet and loamy. Breakfast may be bought at a French-style bistro, or at the dusty Barnyard Farmstall, where hens roost inside the shop among the straw bales and the potatoes. Porcupines still snuffle round gardens after dark, and a genet or even a lynx may occasionally be seen in the vicinity of **Cecilia Forest** (OVERLEAF). At night, owls hoot in the trees and the skies are brilliant with stars, thanks to the absence of street lights.

KIRSTENBOSCH
TO DEVIL'S PEAK

The eastern flank of the mountain is dominated by the vast Groote Schuur Estate, Kirstenbosch National Botanical Garden, Rhodes Memorial and the University of Cape Town. Wildebeest and antelope graze peacefully in the rosy morning light on **Devil's Peak** (ABOVE), unaware of the strange contrast they present to commuters on the five-lane highway below: a quiet nature study on one hand and the sprawling bulk of the world-renowned Groote Schuur Hospital complex on the other.

Kirstenbosch

Kirstenbosch National Botanical Garden was established in 1913 and shaped by Professor Pearson whose gravestone bears the fitting epitaph, 'If ye seek his monument, look around.' The garden is high on visitors' 'must do' lists. Favourites include the Cycad Amphitheatre and The Dell where four clear springs fill a delicate bird-shaped pool. Manicured lawns, vast shady trees, restaurants and **summer concerts** (ABOVE, RIGHT) make it a much-loved local haunt too. Skeleton Gorge trail starts here, and other paths wind through the 36-ha garden cultivated to showcase the diversity of the region's indigenous plants (PREVIOUS SPREAD).

For historians there's the elegant camphor avenue planted by Rhodes in 1898, and the remnants of the wild almond hedge that demarcated the boundary of the Cape settlement in 1660. Van Riebeeck intended it to deter marauding Khoisan; today, in a garden that is ever evolving, the wisdom of the country's many cultures is on display in the Useful Plants Garden. A traditional **Xhosa/Mpondo hut** (ABOVE, LEFT) stands among the shrubs whose medicinal properties have been understood by local healers for centuries.

Rhodes Memorial

Cecil John Rhodes, Prime Minister of the Cape Colony in the last years of the 19th century, was a larger-than-life character who left his stamp all over Africa. Revered by the early British settlers for his dynamism and reviled in post-apartheid South Africa for his colonial racism, the legacy of Rhodes is hard to ignore. His memorial, built on the slopes where he loved to sit, was designed by Sir Herbert Baker and inscribed by his friend Rudyard Kipling. Its proportions reflect the impact of the man known as the 'Colossus of Africa'.

Visitors enjoy the bronze lions and the panoramic view of the city, and hikers often choose the trail from the parking lot as a preferred route to the King's blockhouse on the hill.

Rhodes is commemorated in street names, a keenly contested scholarship, Rhodes University at Grahamstown, and in neighbouring Zimbabwe, previously known as Rhodesia. His memorial overlooks the **University of Cape Town** (PREVIOUS SPREAD), where the impressive façade of Jameson Hall echoes the soaring buttresses of its mountain backdrop.

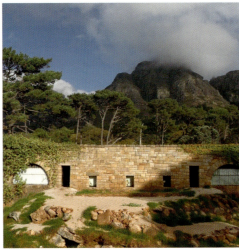

Groote Schuur Estate

Kirstenbosch and **Groote Schuur Hospital** (ABOVE, RIGHT) form part of this estate, which was owned by Rhodes and bequeathed to the people of Cape Town on his death. Rhodes was believed to have introduced the Himalayan tahr to Table Mountain, but was not in fact responsible for this environmental faux pas. In 1936 a pair of animals escaped from the zoo that once stood on the estate. They bred so prolifically that the colony numbered about 600 by the late 1970s. Despite a public outcry, the tahrs were destroyed in order to preserve the natural balance of vegetation on the mountain.

People living near the zoo were accustomed to hearing the lions roar, but today their **enclosure** (ABOVE, CENTRE) is deserted. Antelope frequent the hillside around Rhodes Memorial, and can be seen roaming with wildebeest and zebra on the exposed slopes of **the estate** (OPPOSITE). A project to reintroduce the quagga, now thought to be a subspecies of the Plains zebra, has attracted world-wide attention. Through a careful breeding programme scientists hope that an animal extinct for more than 100 years will re-emerge.

INDEX

Please note: Page numbers in *italics* refer to photographs.

A

Adderley Street 26, *26*
African (Jackass) penguin 84, *85*
alien vegetation *see* vegetation
almond hedge, wild 112
antelope 109, 118
Argus Cycle Tour 98
art/craft
  collectables 90
  route 61
Asian slaves 86
Atlantic seaboard 35, 36

B

baboons 69
 Chacma 78, *78*
 monitors 69
Bain, Thomas 45
Baker, Sir Herbert 116
Bakoven 35, 44, *44–45*
Barnyard Farmstall 105
bathing boxes 94, *95*
Bergvliet 103
birdlife 105
Blouberg 41
Bo-Kaap 17, 26, *27*
books, antiquarian 90
Bottlenosed dolphins 92
Boulders 83, 84, *84*, 85
Boyes Drive 90, 94, *94*
Bryde's whales 92
Buitenverwagting *102*, 103

C

Cableway, Table Mountain Aerial *19*, 20
  restaurant 23, *23*
camel rides 61
Camel Rock 69
camphor avenue 112
Camps Bay 35, *40*, *41–42*
canons 55, *55*
Cape Agulhas 75
Cape Doctor 22
Cape Dutch style 97, 103
Cape Floral Kingdom 32
Cape Hangklip 83
Cape of Good Hope 17, 72, 75–76
Cape of Storms 59
Cape Point 45, *70–71*, 83
 caves *74–75*, 75
Cecilia Forest 105, *106–107*
Chapman, John 53
Chapman's Chaunce *see* Hout Bay
Chapman's Peak *52–53*, 56, *56*
 Drive 53
 toll road 56
charter boats 31
Chart farm 105, *105*
Circle of Islam 17
City Bowl 26
Clifton 35, 38, *38–39*
 Beach 36, *37*
Cloud of Magellan 22
Common dolphins 92
Company Gardens 26
concerts, summer 112, *112*
Constantia 103, 105
 Valley *96–97*, 96–107

Constantiaberg 97, 100, *101*
cruises, harbour and sunset 31
Cycad Amphitheatre 112
cycling 55, 98

D

da Gama, Vasco 72, *72*
Dalebrook tidal pool 90
dassie *see* rock hyrax
Dell, The 112
de Saldanha, Admiral Antonia 20
Devil's Peak 24, 26, *108–109*, 109
De Waterkant 26
Dias, Bartolomeu 17, 71
  cross commemorating *72*
Dias Beach *76–77*
dolphins 31, 92
  Bottlenosed 92
  Common 92
  Dusky 92
Donkin, Sir Rufane 35
Drake, Sir Francis 71
Dusky dolphins 92
Dutch East India Company 17

E

Elephant's Eye *96–97*
Empire Theatre 94

F

False Bay 75, *82–83*, 82–95
farmstall 61
ferries 31
fire
  fighting 32

Silvermine 98
Fish Hoek 88
　beach 83
fishermen 83, 90
fishing
　boats 55, *55*
　trek 86, *88–89*
Flying Dutchman 75
fynbos *see* vegetation

G

gallery, Natale Labia 94
game viewing 61
Garden, Useful Plants 112
Gardens, The 26
genets 105
Glen 36
golf course 100
Gordon's Bay 83
Government Avenue 26
Great White sharks 83, 89
Groot Constantia 103
Groote Schuur
　Estate 109, 118
　Hospital 109, 118, *118*
guesthouses and B&Bs 68

H

harbour 31, *31*
Herodotus 71
Het Posthuys Theatre 94, *94*
hiking
　Cape of Good Hope 72
　Hoerikwaggo (Table Mountain)
　　13, 20
　Lion's Head 36
　Table Mountain Reserve 72
Himalayan Tahr 118
horses *60*, 61
Hout Bay 45, 53, *54*, 55, *55*

Humpback whales 92

I

Imhoff farm 61
Imizamo Yethu (Mandela Park) 55
Indian Ocean 75
Indians 86
Islam 17, 46, *see also* Circle of Islam

J

Jackass penguin *see* African penguin
Jameson Hall 116
Jubilee Square 86
Just Nuisance, Great Dane 86

K

Kaharuddin, Sultan 75
Kalk Bay 90, *91*
　harbour 83
kaolin mine 59
Khoisan 17, 51, 112
　slaves 86
Killer whales 92
King's blockhouse 24, 116
Kipling, Rudyard 116
Kirstenbosch 112
　National Botanical Garden 109,
　　110–111, 112
kite-surfing 42
Klein Constantia 103
Kloof Road 41
Kommetjie 53, *64–65*
kramat *16*, 17

L

Lady Smith's Pass (Kloof Road) 41
leopard, sculpted 55
lighthouse 72, *73*
　Nelson's Rock 86
　Slangkop *62–63*, 64
Lion's Head 17, *18*, *14–15*, 36, *36*

hiking 36
　paragliding 35, 42
Lithuanian Jews 86
Llandudno 35, 45, *48–49*
Logie's Rock Cave 51
lynx 105

M

Mandela Park *see* Imizamo Yethu
marine life 46
medicinal plants 112
Michelse, Matthys 100
milkwood trees 46
Misty Cliffs settlement 65, *66–67*
mongoose, grey 78
Mons Mensa ('table mountain') 22
Mount Nelson Hotel 26, *26*>
Museums
　Het Posthuys 94, *94*
　Simon's Town 86
Muizenberg *82–83*, 83, 94

N

Natale Labia gallery 94
national parks 24, 32
naval base 86
Nelson Mandela Gateway *28–29*, 31
Nelson's Rock lighthouse 86
Newlands forestry station 32
Noordhoek 53, *58–59*, *58–59*
　Valley 61, 98
Noorul Mubeen, Sheik 46
nudist beach 50

O

oil spill 84
ostriches 78, *80–81*
Oudekraal 46, *47*
Ou Kaapse Weg 98, *99*
owls, night 105

P

paragliding 35, 42
Pearson, Professor 112
penguins 83, 84, *85*
pipe track 42, *43*
porcupines 105
potters 61
Pringle Bay 83

Q

quagga 118
Quay Four 31

R

railway 92, *92*
Residency, The *see* Museum, Simon's Town
restaurants
 Kalk Bay 88
 Table Mountain 23
Rhodes, Cecil John 94, 112, 116, 118
Rhodes Memorial 109, 116, *117*, 118
Robben Island 13, 31
rock hyrax (dassie) 23
Round House 41
Rossouw, Frederik 100

S

sailboarding 64, *66–67*
Sandy Bay 50–51, *50–51*
Scarborough 53, 68–69, *68–69*
seabirds *76–77*
seals 78, 83
Sentinel *54*
settlers 86
sharks, Great White 83, 89
shell midden 51
Signal Hill 26, 36
Silvermine Nature Reserve 59, 98, *98*
Simon's Town 83, 84, *87*

Museum 86
Skeleton Gorge trail 112
Slangkop Lighthouse *62–63*
slaves 17, 46, 86
smallpox 51
Solele Buffalo Reserve 61
Somerset, Governor Sir Charles 41
Southern Cross 22
Southern Right whales 83, 92
squatter community 55
Steenberg 100, 103, *103*
 golf course 100, *100*
St James 92, *92*, *93*
Suikerbossie hill 55, *55*
Sunny Cove 89
surf kites 35

T

Table Bay 31
Table Mountain *12–13*, 13, 20
 Aerial Cableway *see under* Cableway
 floodlit at night *14–15*
 National Park 32, 61, 72
 sandstone 45
Tafelberg Road 24
Theatre, Empire 94
tidal pools
 Kalk Bay 88
 St James 92, *93*
tortoise 78
trek fishing 88, *88–89*
Twelve Apostles 35

U

Uitsig 103
Ukuvuka, Operation Firestop 32
Umlindi Wemingizimu (Table Mountain) 13
University of Cape Town 109, *114–115*, 116

Useful Plants Garden 112

V

van der Stel, Simon 103
Van Hunks 24
van Riebeeck, Jan 17, 41, 53, 112
vegetation
 alien 32, 65
 erica 78, *78*, 98
 fynbos 32, 42, 98
 indigenous *110–111*, 112
 invasive 98
 medicinal plants 112
Victoria and Alfred (V & A) Waterfront 13, 31, *31*, 39
Victoria, Queen 45
Victoria Road 45
vineyards 97, 100, 105
von Kamptz, Frederik Ernst 41

W

Wernich, John Lodewyk 41
wetland 61
whales 92
 Bryde's 92
 Humpback 92
 Killer 92
 Southern Right 83, 92
wildebeest 109, 118
wine route 105
Witsand 64, *64–65*

X

Xhosa/Mpondo hut 112, *112*

Y

Yusuf, Sheik 17

Z

zebra 118

First published in 2005 by Struik Publishers (a division of New Holland Publishing (South Africa) (Pty) Ltd)

New Holland Publishing is a member of Johnnic Communications Ltd

Garfield House, 86–88 Edgware Road, London W2 2EA, United Kingdom
www.newhollandpublishers.com

80 McKenzie Street, Cape Town 8001, South Africa
www.struik.co.za

14 Aquatic Drive, Frenchs Forest, NSW 2086, Australia

218 Lake Road, Northcote, Auckland, New Zealand

Copyright © in published edition 2005: Struik Publishers
Copyright © in photographs 2005: Christiaan Diedericks
Copyright © in text 2005: Catherine Eden

ISBN 1 77007 144 X

10 9 8 7 6 5 4 3 2 1

Publishing Manager: Dominique le Roux
Managing Editor: Lesley Hay-Whitton
Senior Designer: Sian Marshall
Proofreader: Helen de Villiers
Indexer: Ethné Clarke
Reproduction by Hirt & Carter Cape (Pty) Ltd
Printed and bound by Craft Print International Ltd

All rights reserved. No part of this publication may be reproduced, stored in a retrieval system or transmitted, in any form, or by any means, electronic, mechanical, photocopying, recording or otherwise, without the prior written permission of the copyright owner(s).

Log on to our photographic website www.imagesofafrica.co.za for an African experience.

Acknowlegments

Sixteen years ago, Fanie Kloppers and Coco encouraged me to follow my dream of becoming a photographer. Thanks to them and to André, Adriaan, Dewald, Tracy, Lynda, Carel, Renée and Bonny for their support. Special thanks to my wonderful friend and writer, Cathy Eden. Each destination visited over the course of our professional association has delivered its jewels, but documenting our home town has proved to be the greatest delight and privilege. Thank you to the team at Struik for making the project possible, and to all those who contributed to the process by supplying information or helping us get where we needed to be: officers of Table Mountain National Park; the Hout Bay Museum; The Slave & Exile History Project of the Simon's Town Museum; Steenberg Golf Estate; Professor Andy Smith; The Table Mountain Aerial Cableway; The Waterfront Boat Company (021 418 5806); Tigger 2 Charters, Hout Bay (021 790 5256); and Dave Hurwitz of the Simon's Town Boat Company (083 257 7760) who made a special trip to Cape Point to accommodate us. CHRISTIAAN DIEDERICKS

  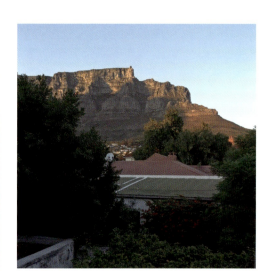

Through the photographer's window

Christiaan Diedericks and Cathy Eden have worked together as a successful team since 1996, covering everything from a wedding at the Taj Mahal to a cloudburst in the Namib Desert. They have seen much of the world, but choose to live and work in the shadow of Table Mountain.